MAKE
FELT
FLOWERS

*Four Seasons of Crafting
Modern Plants & Flowers*

BRYANNE RAJAMANNAR

an imprint of C&T Publishing

PUBLISHER: Amy Barrett-Daffin

CREATIVE DIRECTOR: Gailen Runge

SENIOR EDITOR: Roxane Cerda

EDITOR: Madison Moore

COVER/BOOK DESIGNER: April Mostek

PRODUCTION COORDINATOR: Tim Manibusan

ILLUSTRATOR: Aliza Shalit

PHOTOGRAPHY COORDINATOR: Rachel Ackley

FRONT COVER PHOTOGRAPHY by Gailen Runge of C&T Publishing, Inc.

LIFESTYLE PHOTOGRAPHY by Siobhán Egan and Bevin Valentine Jalbert, Paprika Southern, LLC; INSTRUCTIONAL PHOTOGRAPHY by Bryanne Rajamannar, unless otherwise noted

Published by Stash Books, an imprint of C&T Publishing, Inc., P.O. Box 1456, Lafayette, CA 94549

Library of Congress Cataloging-in-Publication Data

Names: Rajamannar, Bryanne, author.

Title: Make felt flowers : four seasons of crafting modern plants & flowers / Bryanne Rajamannar.

Description: Lafayette, CA : Stash Books, [2023] | Summary: "Learn to create lovely felt flower arrangements. Included inside are easy-to-follow instructions for cutting the felt from simple patterns, assembling the flowers, and polishing them up into detailed bouquets and projects, which include accessories, home decor, and floral gifts for year round"-- Provided by publisher.

Identifiers: LCCN 2023014387 | ISBN 9781644034088 (trade paperback) | ISBN 9781644034095 (ebook)

Subjects: LCSH: Fabric flowers. | Felt work.

Classification: LCC TT890.5 .R35 2023 | DDC 745.594/3--dc23/eng/20230405

LC record available at https://lccn.loc.gov/2023014387

Printed in China

10 9 8 7 6 5 4 3 2 1

DEDICATION

Dedicated to Kumar, Sienna, and Mira, my truest loves.

ACKNOWLEDGMENTS

It has taken a remarkable amount of time and effort, by many people, to get this book in your hands. I cannot thank the entire team at C&T Publishing enough for turning my work into this finished book. Special thanks to Madison Moore at C&T Publishing, for leading me through this endeavor throughout its many phases. Thank you to Bevin Jalbert and Siobhan Egan at Paprika Southern for gracing this project with beautiful imagery through their photography and styling.

Thank you to my friends and family for your unending support. A huge and heartfelt thank you to my Mom for stepping in to lend a hand and cheer me on, through this and all things. And, thank you to Kumar, Sienna, and Mira, for loving me whether I'm writing a book or not.

Contents

85

88

91

95

98

101

104

107

110

114

117

Introduction

Hello, and welcome!

Thank you so much for purchasing this book! I have so enjoyed sharing this craft with you, through my first book, *Felt Flower Workshop: A Modern Guide to Crafting Gorgeous Plants and Flowers from Fabric*, and I can't wait for you to explore this new batch of projects. Seeing your creations over the last couple of years has been so rewarding and inspiring. In this book, we'll work through the four seasons to create an array of blooms and foliage suitable for any time of year.

My love for creating felt flowers is more than eleven years strong. What began as a way to create hair accessories for my first daughter and accents for my sister's wedding has bloomed into a passion for creating flowers of all shapes, sizes, colors, and types. All these years, an online shop, brick-and-mortar storefront and workspace, and two books later, I am in awe of how this beautiful journey has unfolded. Being able to delve into the beauty of nature and immerse myself in the creative process is such a joyful gift for me. I hope that you, too, find this to be a rewarding, fun, and fulfilling hobby.

Using This Book

This book is divided into two main parts: individual flowers and projects. Through the flower tutorials, you'll learn, step by step, how to create individual flowers, plants, and greenery stems. Then you'll combine different flowers and leaves to create a variety of floral projects to adorn your home, an event, and even yourself!

Getting Started

I love making felt flowers because you can get started with just a few simple and inexpensive supplies. If you're an avid crafter, you probably already have most of these items on hand. Anything you don't have is easy to find at your local craft store or online.

TOOLS & MATERIALS

Hot Glue Guns & Glue Sticks

I recommend using a low-temperature glue gun. I've used high-temperature glue guns, and while they work great, burns and blisters are an unwelcome side effect. You can achieve a strong bond on felt with low-temperature hot glue. I also like to use a mini glue gun because it's easy to hold and doesn't get in the way while working on small details.

Pliers & Wire Cutters

A multi-tool with both needle-nose and wire-snipping components (like those used for jewelry making) is great, but you can also use two separate tools. You'll use these to bend and cut floral wire.

Scissors

At least one sharp pair of fabric scissors is a must—dull scissors on felt are a nightmare! I particularly like scissors with a razor edge. If your scissors are sharp enough, you can cut through multiple layers of felt with relative ease.

Felt

There are more varieties of felt than you may realize! Any felt can be used to make the flowers in this book. Still, the type you choose can significantly affect your project's outcome, mainly because some felts are better quality than others.

Craft Felt. This is the most common and easy-to-find type of felt. It's probably what you remember from your childhood crafts. It's made of synthetic fibers, is easily accessible, and comes in a variety of colors. Though you can certainly make your flowers with this felt, your blooms will be a bit lower quality.

Wool-Blend Felt. Wool-blend felt is a blend of wool and rayon. It's considered an heirloom-quality felt and resists pilling. I made all of the flowers in this book using wool-blend felt. It's easy to work with, comes in beautiful colors, is durable, and is reasonably priced. Wool-blend felt can also stand up to the heat of an iron if you need to smooth out some of your pieces. This felt is easy to find online on marketplaces like Etsy and is starting to show up in craft and fabric stores, available by the yard.

100% Wool Felt. As the name implies, this felt is made entirely of wool. It's more expensive and is usually thicker than wool-blend. It's also a beautiful product that is still suitable for creating flowers. However, results will vary based on type and thickness.

Felt Balls, Pom-Poms & Shapes

Felt balls, pom-poms, and shapes (like the bees on the Spring Wreath, page 85) are wet-felted or needle-felted shapes that can add something fun to your creations. The balls come in a variety of sizes and are great for flower centers, berries, or anytime a perfectly smooth, round surface is desired. The little felt shapes, also available online, are the perfect way to add that something extra to your projects.

Floral Wire

When it comes to floral wire, the lower the gauge, the thicker the wire. Cloth-wrapped wires ensure that the textile look of the flowers is maintained all the way through the stem.

Green, Cloth-Wrapped, 18-Gauge Wire. This gauge is ideal for flower stems. It can support the weight of the flower blooms while still offering some movement. Most (if not all) floral wire comes packaged in 18″ pieces.

Green, Cloth-Wrapped, 20- or 22-Gauge Wire. Because this wire is thinner than 18-gauge wire, it's easy to manipulate and twist. It's ideal for wrapping around other pieces of wire.

Bark-Wrapped Coiled Wire. This natural-looking wire can be wrapped in bark or paper and makes an excellent base for flower crowns and garlands.

Twine

Jute or hemp twine has many uses, from tying on wreath attachments to holding together a bouquet. It's a natural and neutral material that blends well with the other materials you'll use for flower-making.

Fabric Stiffener Spray

Fabric stiffener, like Aileen's Stiffen Quick Spray, is perfect for shaping felt petals and leaves. You can use it to curl long leafy tendrils and to crease or crinkle petals, adding dimension and giving them a more realistic look. It also helps give strength and structure to larger petals and leaves.

Pigments

Markers, acrylic paint, chalk, pastels, and regular makeup can add depth and detail to your florals. Different pigment sources work best for different effects. For sharp lines and dots, fabric markers work well. For soft, blended colors, a powdered pigment is best. Powdered potential sources of color include chalk, chalk pastels, and powdered makeup like eyeshadows and blushes. Acrylic paint gives an opaque color and can also add stiffness if desired.

Wool Roving

Roving is soft, fluffy wool that has been (sometimes) dyed and is used in wet felting and needle felting. So, it's what wool felt is before it's felted into flat sheets! While we aren't needle felting or wet felting in this book, I do use roving in some projects. It's a great complement to flat felt for covering objects, filling gaps, and adding softness.

USING TEMPLATES

At the back of the book, you'll find templates for each of the leaves and flowers. You can use these as exact patterns or just as visual guides. Here are several options for working with the templates.

Make Reusable templates

Place a piece of tracing paper over a template from the book and trace it. Cut out the paper shape and trace it onto cardstock. Make sure to use paper scissors—not your fabric ones! Cut out the cardstock shape, and you now have a reusable template to trace onto felt over and over. You could also cut the template pages and shapes directly out of the book, but be sure you don't lose them!

Make Iron-on templates

Place a piece of wax or freezer paper over a template from the book and trace it. Iron the paper directly onto the felt, wax-side down at low heat. Important: Test the heat on scrap felt before using this method; wool or wool-blend felt can be ironed, but other varieties that are completely synthetic may melt under the heat. After ironing the paper to the felt, cut through both the paper and the felt to cut out the shape.

Use the Templates as a Visual Guide

Most of the petals and leaves are made from basic shapes that you may be comfortable drawing or cutting freehand. Use the templates to get an idea of the size and shape of the pieces, and then draw or cut them yourself. A great way to get uniform shapes is to cut multiple pieces at once (see Cutting Multiple Felt Pieces, page 13).

Attach the Stem and Calyx

SUPPLIES

Finished flower

Green felt for calyx

18˝ of 18-gauge floral wire

Calyx template

Needle-nose pliers

Wire cutters

Scissors

Hot glue gun and glue sticks

MAKE THE STEM

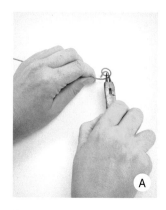

A

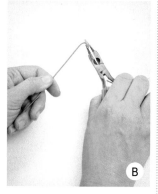

B

STEP 1. Using a pair of needle-nose pliers, shape the wire into a flat coil. For most flowers, a ¾˝ diameter coil works well, but you may have to make the coil larger or smaller depending on the size of the flower. **A**

STEP 2. Bend the wire at a 90° angle to the coil to form a little platform. Push the coil over so it's centered above the stem. **B**

ATTACH THE STEM AND CALYX

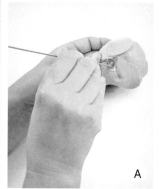

A

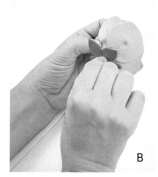

B

STEP 1. Add a generous amount of hot glue (a circle a bit larger than the coil) to the bottom of the flower, and press the coil onto it. **A**

STEP 2. Cut a felt calyx large enough to cover the wire coil and the bottom of the flower. Cut a tiny slit into the center of the calyx and slide it up the stem. Press the calyx into the glue, covering the wire coil. Glue down any loose edges. You may need to add additional glue to the calyx to attach it securely. **B**

Cut Multiple Felt Pieces

When cutting multiple leaves or petals of the same shape,
this technique will save you time and hand fatigue! Rather than cutting
each piece individually, you can cut multiple, almost identical pieces at once.
You can use one of the templates provided as a guide or cut freehand.

STEP 1. Prepare the felt. Cut a long strip of felt that's about as wide as the leaves or petals are long. Fold over the felt to double or triple it, so you'll be cutting through multiple layers (make sure your scissors are sharp!). Cut the felt into rectangles about the same width as the leaves or petals. **A**

STEP 2. Cut the leaves or petals. Stack two or three rectangles together and cut out the leaf or petal shape. To quickly cut leaves, round off the top right corner, then rotate the rectangles 180° and repeat. Continue cutting leaves or petals from the remaining rectangles. **B**

SPRING

Icelandic Poppy

These bright beauties are so cheerful! Their tropical colors exude springtime warmth and light, breezy vibes. I think they look best in bunches of mixed colors.

SUPPLIES

9″ x 12″ sheet of peach felt (or another bright, warm color)

1″ x 6″ strip of yellow felt

½″ bright green felt pom-pom

Icelandic poppy templates (page 122)

1 piece 18″ long of 18-gauge cloth-covered floral wire

Scissors

Hot glue gun and glue sticks

Fabric stiffener

CUT PIECES

Follow the template to cut out:

6 peach petals

2 green leaves

1 green calyx

CONSTRUCT THE FLOWER

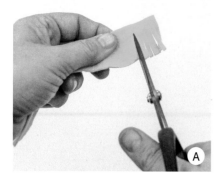

STEP 1. Cut small slits along one edge of the yellow felt to create a fringe. Cut somewhere between halfway and two-thirds of the way across the strip. Don't cut all the way through. **A**

STEP 2. Put a small drop of glue on one end of the yellow felt strip, along the bottom (uncut) edge. Wrap the strip around the center of the felt pom-pom, adding more glue to attach as you go. **B-C**

STEP 3. Cut a ½˝ slit in the bottom of each petal. Apply glue to one side of the slit and overlap the pieces to give the petals a cupped shape. **D**

STEP 4. Add glue to the front base of one petal, and press it onto the underside of the flower center. Repeat to attach the first three petals, spacing them evenly around the center. **E-F**

STEP 5. Repeat Step 4 to add the remaining three petals around the flower. Stagger them between and behind the first three. **G**

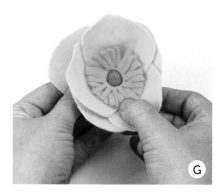

ADD DETAIL AND TEXTURE

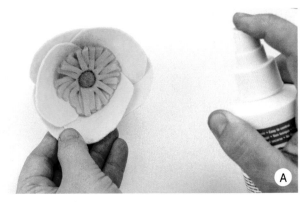

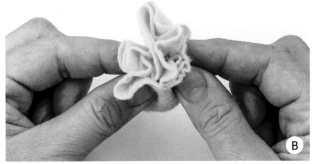

STEP 1. Spray the flower liberally with fabric stiffener, and then squish the petals together with your fingertips. Repeat several times to give them the signature crinkled look of a poppy. **A-B**

STEP 2. Using your fingertips, gently open up the flower, being careful not to lose the texture. Reposition any of the yellow stamens that may have been smushed in the process. **C**

C

STEM, CALYX, AND LEAVES

A

STEP 1. To add a stem, calyx, and leaves to the Icelandic poppy, see Attach the Stem and Calyx (page 12). **A**

Stargazer Lily

These stunning members of the Oriental hybrid lily family are a favorite. They have huge, colorful blossoms, intense color, and a sweet fragrance. However, if you're an allergy sufferer, you may have found out the hard way that these aren't the best choice for the center of your table...unless, of course, you make your own from felt! No pollen, no problem.

SUPPLIES

9˝ x 12˝ white or light pink felt

2˝ x 2˝ dark orange or copper-colored felt

½˝ square of light green felt

Stargazer templates (page 126)

6 pieces 5˝ each of 24-gauge cloth-wrapped floral wire

1 piece 18˝ long of 18-gauge cloth-wrapped floral wire

Scissors

Hot glue gun and glue sticks

Dark pink pigment (See Pigments, page 10)

Brush

CUT PIECES

Follow the template to cut out:

6 petals from the pink or white felt

6 ovals from the copper or dark orange felt

1 small circle (about ¼˝ diameter) and 1 calyx from the green felt

CONSTRUCT THE FLOWER

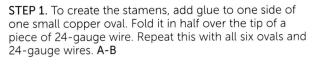

STEP 1. To create the stamens, add glue to one side of one small copper oval. Fold it in half over the tip of a piece of 24-gauge wire. Repeat this with all six ovals and 24-gauge wires. **A-B**

STEP 2. Add a petal to the opposite end of each of the same six wires. Add a thin line of hot glue all the way down the center of a petal, starting about 1½˝ from the tip. Place the wire onto the glue. Fold the petal in half around the wire and glue. Hold for a few seconds to let the glue set. The wire shouldn't be visible in the middle of the petal. If it is, touch it up by adding more glue to the visible areas, or remelting the glue with the tip of your glue gun, and pressing the petal together more tightly. **C-D**

STEP 3. At the base of each petal on the back side, put a tiny dot of glue on either side of the wire, and fold the sides of the petal back. This will keep the petal open. **E-F**

STEP 4. Brush color onto each petal. This can be done with colored chalk, pan pastels, or even eyeshadow and blush. Stargazers can vary in terms of how intense their color is and how much of the petal it covers. For my flowers, I'm covering almost the entire petal in a deep pink eyeshadow, leaving only the edges white, for a bolder look. **G**

STEP 5. Glue the small green circle to the tip of the 18-gauge stem wire. Fold it down around the stem. **H**

STEP 6. Hold all six stamen and petal pairs together around the stem. Using one of the stamen wires, wrap the stem around the entire group of wires to secure. Do this as close to the bottom as possible. **I**

STEP 7. Move the petals out of the way and add the calyx. Slide it up the stem and glue it into place below the petals, adding enough glue that the calyx grabs onto the base of the petals and wires. Hold until it's secure. This will give the flowers some stability and help stop the petals from sliding all over. **J**

STEP 8. Begin positioning the petals. Put some glue at the base of a petal and fold it up toward the center wires. Hold until the glue is set. This should pull the center of the flower in tighter. Repeat with two more petals, selecting in total three alternating petals.

STEP 9. Glue up the remaining three petals. They should be slightly behind the first three and staggered in between. **K**

STEP 10. Shape the flower by bending a curve into each of the petals. **L**

Claire de Lune Peony

When thinking of peonies, most people picture the densely packed petals and rounded shape of other varieties. The Claire de Lune, however, is characterized by its big, bold, yellow center and delicate white petals. Eye-catching and graceful, this bloom looks great alongside other flowers in arrangements, with other Claire de Lunes, or as a single stem elegantly displayed in a vase.

SUPPLIES

9″ x 1½″ yellow felt

9″ x 12″ white felt

3″ x 6″ green felt

Claire de Lune templates (page 126)

1 piece 18″ long of 18-gauge cloth-wrapped floral wire

Scissors

Hot glue gun and glue sticks

CUT PIECES

Follow the template to cut out

3 petal size A in white felt

3 petal size B in white felt

2 leaves and 1 calyx in green felt

CONSTRUCT THE FLOWER

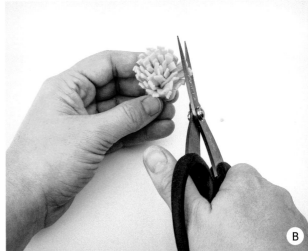

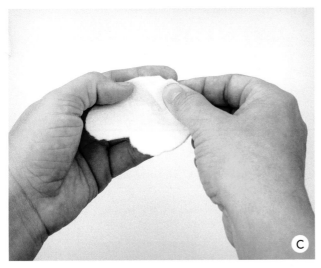

STEP 1. Cut a small ½″ slit into the bottom (the flat end) of all six petals.

STEP 2. Cut small slits along one side of the yellow felt. The slits should approximately be ⅛″ apart and ½″ long.

STEP 3. Glue along the uncut, bottom edge of the strip and roll it up to create a fluffy yellow center. Glue a bit, then roll, then add more glue until the whole strip has been rolled up. **A**

STEP 4. Trim the center into a dome shape. **B**

STEP 5. Put a small dot of hot glue on one side of the slit on the bottom of a petal, and overlap the pieces to give the petals a cupped shape. It doesn't matter which side ends up on top. **C**

STEP 6. Hold the petal, positioning your thumbs in the very center. Stretch the felt a few times to make the curve more distinct. Repeat with all six petals, careful to keep the smaller ones separate from the larger ones. **D**

STEP 7. Put glue on the front base of one of the smaller petals, and press it onto the underside of the flower center. **E-F**

STEP 8. Repeat with the other two small petals, evenly spacing them around the center. Then add the remaining three petals, staggering them between and behind the first three. **G**

STEM, CALYX, AND LEAVES

STEP 1. To add a stem, calyx, and leaves to the Claire de Lune Peony, see Attach the Stem and Calyx (page 12). **A**

Daffodil

Daffodils are a telltale sign that spring has arrived. These iconic blooms have most commonly been yellow in years past. However, today, newer cultivars are springing up in a variety of peaches, golds, and creams, giving these traditional beauties an updated color palette and a fresh new look.

SUPPLIES

2″ × 2½″ gold felt

4″ × 8″ peach or yellow felt

2″ × 4″ green felt

Daffodil templates (page 121)

1 piece 18″ long of 18-gauge cloth-covered floral wire

Scissors

Hot glue gun and glue sticks

CUT PIECES

Follow the template to cut out

2 petal shapes from peach or yellow felt

Calyx from green felt

CONSTRUCT THE FLOWER

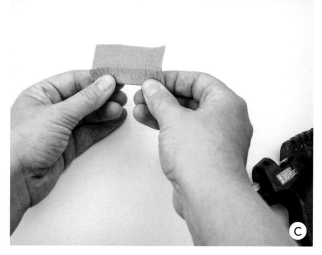

STEP 1. Cut a small slit, just big enough to fit a piece of wire through, in the middle of each of the two petal pieces. Set aside.

STEP 2. Cut ¼˝ slits along one of the longer sides of the center shape, spacing the cuts about ⅛˝ to ¼˝ apart. **A**

STEP 3. Measure ¾˝ from the fringe edge toward the middle of the felt piece, and run a line of glue all the way across. **B**

STEP 4. Fold the fringe up along the glue line. **C**

STEP 5. Add glue along one of the short sides of the center piece. Bring the other side around and press together to make a tube. The fringe should be on the inside of the tube. **D-E**

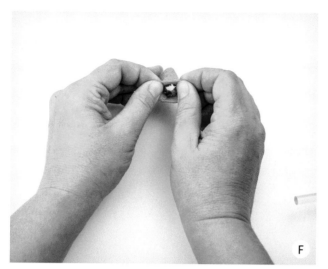

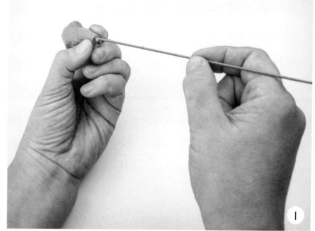

STEP 6. Along the unfolded edge of the tube, begin stretching the felt. Hold the felt between your fingers and pull. You'll need to pull pretty hard to separate the fibers a bit. Do this repeatedly, working your way around the top of the daffodil center. This creates a ruffled effect. **F-G**

STEP 7. Apply glue around the folded bottom edge of the daffodil center, and insert the end of the floral wire. Press the felt around the wire and hold until the glue sets. **H-I**

TIP

If you use too much glue when attaching the center to the wire, it will squeeze up into the flower center and be visible or out the bottom and burn your fingers. Try for a light, even coverage along the very edge for best results. This might take a couple of tries, and that's okay!

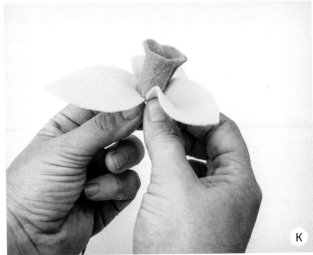

STEP 8. Slide one of the petal pieces onto the wire through the small slit. Add glue to the middle of the petal piece when it's close to the flower center, and then press it into place. **J**

STEP 9. Add a dot of glue to the base of one petal segment, and pinch the base of the petal as you press it close to the flower center to create a small pucker. Repeat on the other three petal segments. **K**

STEP 10. Repeat steps 8 and 9 with the second petal piece. Stagger this petal between and behind the first set so all the petals are showing. **L-M**

STEM, CALYX, AND LEAVES

STEP 1. To add a stem, calyx, and leaves to the daffodil, see Attach the Stem and Calyx (page 12).

Jasmine Vines

Springtime is often marked by the unmistakable sweet aroma of jasmine blooms. The vines climb and cover anything standing still and reward us with both adorable white blooms and an intoxicating fragrance. While this felt version won't give you the trademark scent, it will last longer than the fresh version and might just make you feel like spring is sticking around a little longer. Jasmine is also a great way to lighten up an arrangement.

SUPPLIES

6˝ x 9˝ white or off-white felt

6˝ x 9˝ green felt

Jasmine templates (page 123)

5 pieces 8˝ each of 24-gauge cloth-wrapped floral wire

1 piece 18˝ long of 18-gauge cloth-covered floral wire

Scissors

Hot glue gun and glue sticks

CUT PIECES

Follow the template to cut out

5 flower shapes from the white or off-white felt

5 leaf shapes from the green felt

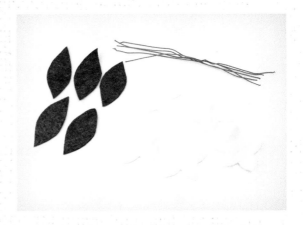

CONSTRUCT THE FLOWER

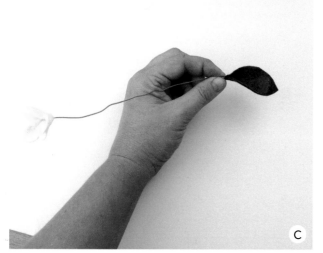

STEP 1. Snip a tiny hole into the center of each flower.

STEP 2. Slide a flower shape onto the end of a piece of 24-gauge wire. Add a tiny dot of hot glue to the center and pinch the flower around the tip of the wire. Try to pinch evenly in all directions so the flower is centered on the stem. Repeat this for all five flower shapes. **A-B**

STEP 3. Add a leaf to each stem, on the opposite side of the wire. Put a very small drop of glue on the tip of a leaf. Pinch the end of the leaf around the tip of the wire and hold until it's secure. **C**

STEP 4. Gather three of the jasmine blooms together and twist their wires around the 18-gauge wire, leaving about 2″ of stem and bloom extending from the end of the heavier wire. **D**

STEP 5. Wrap the remaining two stems of blooms and leaves on the opposite side of the 18-gauge wire, facing the other way. **E**

STEP 6. Spread the blooms apart and position the leaves around the flowers. **F**

STEP 7. Bend the main stem into an arch to replicate a hanging vine. Jasmine isn't a rigid plant. It's a free spirit and has a vine-like nature. It's also loose and drapey (and good for making flower crowns!). **G**

SUMMER

Hibiscus

For tropical vibes, look no further. Nothing says "vacation" like a hibiscus tucked behind your ear or on your table. These showy flowers are a staple in landscapes where I live. But if that's not the case for you, maybe this tutorial will hold you over until your next getaway!

SUPPLIES

6″ x 9″ coral felt (or another bright color)

Small strip of red felt approx. ½″ x ¾″

Small strip of yellow felt approx. ½″ x 1½″

6″ x 9″ green felt

Hibiscus templates (page 121)

1 piece 18″ long of 18-gauge cloth-covered floral wire

Scissors

Hot glue gun and glue sticks

Dark pink or red pigment (see Pigments, page 10)

CUT PIECES

Follow the template to cut out

5 petals from the coral felt

1 calyx from the green felt

1 leaf from the green felt

CONSTRUCT THE FLOWER

STEP 1. To make the center, cut five small slits into the red felt. **A**

STEP 2. Glue and wrap the red felt around the tip of the wire. Hold until the glue cools. **B**

STEP 3. Fringe the yellow felt by making small snips all the way across one long edge, being careful not to cut all the way through to the other edge. Add glue along the bottom, uncut edge, and wrap onto the wire below the red felt. **C**

STEP 4. Add color to the base of each petal, going about ⅓ of the way up, using a small paintbrush or your finger. **D**

STEP 5. Begin attaching the petals directly to the wire, about 1½" below the yellow/red center. Add a touch of glue to the base of the first petal and pinch it around the wire. Angle the petal out so it is opening out from the wire. **E**

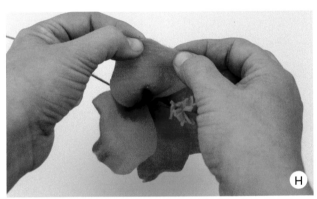

STEP 6. Repeat to add the rest of the petals one at a time. Each petal should slightly overlap the previous petal. Try not to move down the stem as you attach. You want the petals to be as close to the same level around the stem as possible. As you add the final petal, make sure it overlaps in the same way as the previous petals, with one side tucking underneath the first petal, and the other side overlapping the previous petal. Use a little extra glue to hold it into position. **F-G**

STEP 7. Ruffle the edges of each petal by stretching the felt between your fingers, working across the top of each petal. **H**

STEP 8. Snip a tiny hole in the middle of the calyx and slide it up the stem. Glue it to the bottom of the hibiscus bloom. Finally, glue the leaf on, angling it slightly outward, about 2″ to 3″ below the flower. **I-J**

Monstera

The monstera is characterized by large heart-shaped leaves perforated by holes called "fenestration." Now a popular houseplant, it originated in warmer climates and will add a lush summertime feel to your arrangements and projects.

SUPPLIES

9″ x 12″ green felt

Monstera template (page 124)

1 piece 18″ long of 18- or 16-gauge cloth-covered floral wire

4 pieces 4½″ each of 22-gauge cloth-covered floral wire

Hot glue gun and glue sticks

Green pigment (see Pigments, page 10)

CUT PIECES

Follow the template to cut out

1 monstera leaf shape from green felt

TIP

Keep in mind that no one else will see the monstera template, so if your hole placement is a little different, don't worry! No two leaves are alike.

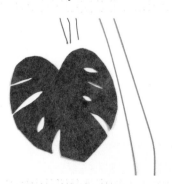

CONSTRUCT THE LEAF

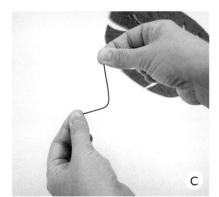

STEP 1. Attach the stem to the leaf. Run a line of glue down the center of the leaf, starting about 2″ from the top. Press the stem wire (18-gauge or 16-gauge) into it and let it dry. **A-B**

STEP 2. Bend the shorter wire pieces in the center and place them onto the back of the leaf along the main stem. Add a dot of glue to the tips and center of each wire to secure it in place. Space all four evenly down the main stem wire. **C-E**

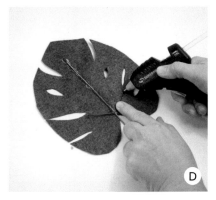

TIP

The back of your leaf will likely end up a gluey mess. You can trim off any big pieces of glue after they've dried to clean it up. Ultimately, however, the back of the leaf won't be visible. If you want to use your leaf in a way that will expose the back, cut two of the same leaf shapes out and glue them together after adding the wire.

ADD DETAIL

STEP 1. Add some detail with color. I used a regular color pencil in yellow-green to define the main stem down the center of the leaf. You can also add some additional veining detail along the sides of the leaf. **A**

STEP 2. Finally, bend the stem so the tip of the leaf is pointing downward. **B**

Hydrangea

Hydrangeas are a Southern landscape staple and an iconic wedding floral. The flower of the hydrangea is actually made up of many florets, or smaller flowers. The key to constructing this flower is to first create all of the florets, then assemble them onto the stem to create that big, puffy, ball-like blossom we all know and love.

SUPPLIES

9″ x 12″ blue or pink felt

6″ x 9″ green felt

Hydrangea templates (page 121)

9 pieces 6″ each of 24-gauge
cloth-covered floral wire

1 piece 18″ long of 18-gauge
cloth-covered floral wire

Scissors

Hot glue gun and glue sticks

CUT PIECES

Follow the template to cut out

19 flower shapes from the blue or pink felt

2 leaves from the green felt

CONSTRUCT THE FLOWER

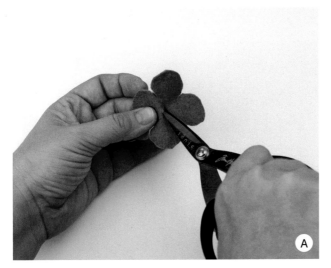

STEP 1. Snip a tiny hole into the center of each flower. **A**

STEP 2. Slide a flower onto the tip of a piece of 24-gauge wire. Add a tiny dot of hot glue to the center and press the petals in toward the wire. After it sets, hold the base of the flower and use your other hand to pull and space the individual petals out. Repeat to add a flower to all nine wire pieces. **B**

STEP 3. Repeat Step 2 to add a second flower on the opposite side of each wire piece. **C**

STEP 4. Attach the remaining flower to the end of the 18-gauge wire. Glue, press, and stretch it the same way. **D**

STEP 5. Begin adding the flower pairs onto the main stem. Wrap the wire of the first one a couple of inches below the flower already attached to the main stem. Wrap once or twice, taking note to position the two flowers at the same height as the center flower. **E**

F

G

H

I

STEP 6. Continue adding the rest of the flower pairs. Wrap them all in approximately the same place. It's okay for the wrapped wires to overlap on top of one another. Be mindful that they're wrapped securely and not loose and wobbly. The tops of the flowers should line up with one another. **F**

STEP 7. Once all of the floret pairs are added, spread them out and position them into a round, domed shape. **G**

STEP 8. Add the leaves. Apply glue to the bottom center of one leaf and press it around the main stem, angling it slightly outward. Repeat with the second leaf on the other side. Position the leaves relatively high on the stem so they curve around the hydrangea flower and cover the twisted wires inside. **H-J**

J

Protea

Proteas have a striking, otherworldly quality. They feature a large round center and sturdy, spiky petals. Adding a protea to a floral arrangement provides instant interest and is eye-catching as a focal flower or accent.

SUPPLIES

9″ x 12″ dark pink felt

9″ x 12″ light pink or peach felt

6″ x 9″ green felt

Protea templates (page 122)

1 piece 18″ long of 18-gauge or 16-gauge cloth-covered floral wire

Scissors

Hot glue gun and glue sticks

Dark pink or red pigment (see Pigment, page 10)

Paintbrush (optional)

2″ diameter Styrofoam ball

CUT PIECES

Follow the template to cut out

14 flower petals from the dark pink felt

25 center shapes from the light pink or peach felt

1 calyx from the green felt

2 leaves from the green felt

CONSTRUCT THE FLOWER

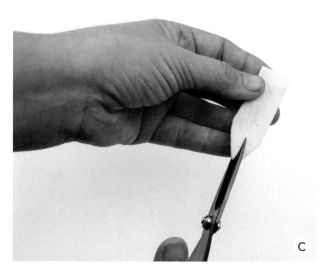

STEP 1. Roll the Styrofoam on the tabletop with the palm of your hand to shape the ball into an elongated shape. Continue shaping to make one end of the oval a little narrower so you have a slight cone shape. Shape between your hands as well. **A-B**

STEP 2. Cut a 1″ slit into the pointed end of each of the center, lighter-colored petals. **C**

STEP 3. Apply glue in a "V" shape onto one petal and press it onto the cone. The flat side of the petal should be toward the narrower end of the cone. The cut side of the petal will be at the top, wider end of the cone. The tips of the petals won't be glued all the way down. They will meet at the top and form a sort of tuft. **D-E**

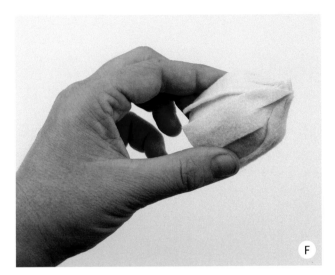

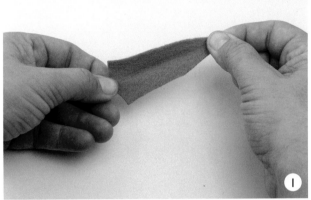

STEP 4. Repeat Step 3 to add about eight petals to cover the foam. Overlap the petals as you go. **F**

STEP 5. Add a second round of eight inner petals. This layer should be slightly lower than the first. Remember, the very tips of these petals are not glued down. **G**

STEP 6. Add the third and final layer of eight inner petals. Again, place them slightly lower than the previous layer. After you have added all the petals, apply extra glue to the bottom of the petals and press around the bottom of the Styrofoam form. Leave the tips unglued. Set aside. **H**

STEP 7. Shape the outer, dark-colored petals by stretching each one with your fingertips. **I**

STEP 8. Put a small dot of glue on the tip of each outer petal, and pinch it together to make a point. **J-K**

STEP 9. Put a 1″ line of glue through the center of the bottom of one outer petal, and add it to the center ball. The petal should be somewhat upright. Be careful not to add glue too high, making the petal curve around the center. You want it poking straight up. **L-M**

STEP 10. Add seven outer petals to the center ball, overlapping them slightly. You may need more or fewer petals; just be sure to go all the way around. **N**

Bottom of protea

STEP 11. Add a second layer of outer petals. These petals are positioned slightly lower than the first layer. The bottoms of the petals will wrap down around the foam. Stagger the petals between and behind the first row of petals. **O**

STEP 12. Add color to the center of the protea with your pigment of choice. I'm using eyeshadow in a deep raisin color. Brush it on with a paintbrush or smudge it in with your finger. **P**

STEM, CALYX, AND LEAVES

STEP 1. To add a stem, calyx, and leaves to the protea, see Attach the Stem and Calyx (page 12). **A**

Palm Fan

Nothing says "summer vacation" like a palm tree. Palm fans can be an interesting accent in a floral design to invoke a tropical feel. When used in other more muted neutrals, palm fans give a natural boho look that can be enjoyed year-round.

SUPPLIES

6″ × 9″ rectangle of sage green felt

¾″ × 5″ strip of sage green felt

Palm Fan template (page 128)

1 piece 18″ long of 18-gauge cloth-wrapped floral wire

Hot glue gun and glue sticks

Fabric stiffener

Small iron or flat iron

Clothespins (optional)

CUT PIECES

Follow the template to cut out

1 palm from the sage green

½″ × 4″ or ¾″ × 5″

CONSTRUCT THE PALM

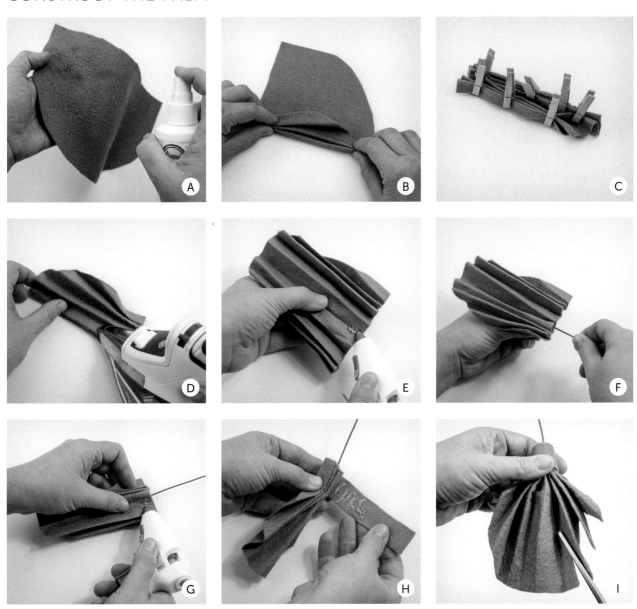

STEP 1. Generously spray the felt pieces with fabric stiffener. **A**

STEP 2. Beginning on one rounded side, fold the felt into ½˝ to ¾˝ sections, back and forth in a repeating accordion fold. **B**

STEP 3. When you've folded all the felt, secure the folds in place. Use clothespins or place the folded felt between two heavy objects while the fabric stiffener dries. **C**

STEP 4. When the felt is fully dry, remove the clips or objects. Use the iron or flat iron to make all the creases deeper. Do this on both sides. **D**

STEP 5. Glue the stem wire into one of the pleats in the center of the felt. **E-F**

STEP 6. Glue all of the pleats together on both the front and back at the base. **G**

STEP 7. Glue and wrap the loose strip of felt around the bottom of the palm to finish the base. **H**

STEP 8. Trim points into the top of the palm. **I**

FALL

Mushroom

Have fun with these fungi! Experiment with different felt ball sizes and proportions. Play around with the colors and accents to make a variety of mushrooms for your projects. Mushrooms have been cropping up all over the place, and this simple tutorial has you covered for crafting all of your tiny mushroom needs.

SUPPLIES

1½″ felt ball in almond or another neutral color

1″ × 12″ strip of light tan felt

1½″ circle of brown felt

2″ piece of 18-gauge wire

Wire cutters

Hot glue gun and glue sticks

Scissors

Brown or black pigment (See Pigments, page 10)

White acrylic paint

Brush

CONSTRUCT THE MUSHROOM

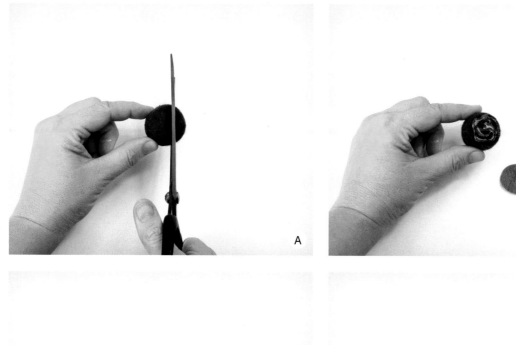

STEP 1. Cut the felt ball with a pair of scissors. Where you cut the ball will determine the shape of the mushroom's cap. You can cut in the middle, but I prefer to cut at about the two-thirds mark. **A**

STEP 2. Add glue to the flat side of the larger piece of the felt ball, and press the brown felt circle onto it. **B-C**

STEP 3. Trim away any brown felt that's hanging over the edge of the felt ball. This is the mushroom cap. **D**

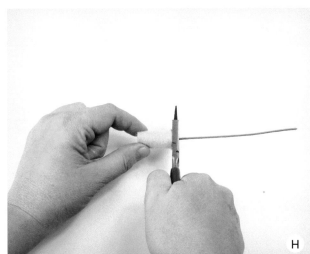

STEP 4. Put a line of glue on one short end of the strip of tan felt. **E**

STEP 5. Wrap the end of the strip around the piece of wire. Roll the felt strip around the wire until you reach the end. Secure the end with more hot glue. **F-G**

STEP 6. Using a pair of wire cutters, snip the wire as close to the bottom of the felt as possible. This is the stem. **H**

STEP 7. Add glue to one end of the stem, and attach it to the bottom of the mushroom cap. **I**

ADD DETAIL

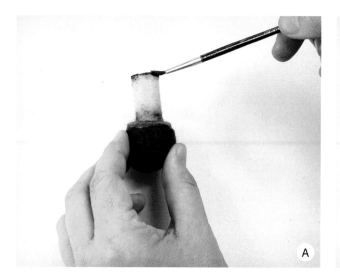

STEP 1. Using the pigment of your choice and a brush or your finger, add a dark color onto the top and bottom of the stem. **A**

STEP 2. Smudge in the color with your fingertips. Remember, mushrooms grow from the ground, so making them look a little dirty is more realistic! **B**

STEP 3. Paint little dots onto the mushroom cap with white acrylic paint. **C**

Café au Lait Dahlia

A plethora of petals, creamy tones mixed with muted neutrals and warm blush accents, a large blossom, and named after a coffee drink—what's not to love? The Café au Lait Dahlia is soft in color but bold in style.

SUPPLIES

¾″ felt ball

9″ x 12″ ivory or cream felt

3″ x 6″ olive green felt

Café au Lait Dahlia templates (pages 126-127)

1 piece 18″ long of 18-gauge cloth-covered floral wire

Hot glue gun and glue sticks

Scissors

Beige powdered pigment (see Pigments, page 10)

Brush (optional)

CUT PIECES

Follow the template to cut out

1 small petal section in ivory or cream felt

2 medium petal sections in ivory or cream felt

2 large petal sections in ivory or cream felt

1 calyx in olive green

1 leaf in olive green

CONSTRUCT THE FLOWER

STEP 1. Apply glue to the center of the small petal section, and press the felt ball into it. **A-B**

STEP 2. Run a line of glue down each of the petal, one at a time, and press onto the ball. **C-D**

STEP 3. Using the pigment of your choice (in my case, beige mineral powder foundation), add pigment to the center of both medium petal sections, not letting the color reach all the way to the tips. **E**

STEP 4. Add one medium petal section to the flower center. Put glue in the center of one medium petal section, and press the ball into it. **F-G**

STEP 5. On the attached medium petal section, add some glue to the bottom of each petal piece. Press again so that the petals are more parallel to the center, not splayed open. **H**

STEP 6. Add glue to the center of the second medium petal section, and attach it to the flower in the same way as Step 4. You don't need to add additional glue to keep the petals upright this time. **I**

STEP 6. On both large petal sections, put a dot of glue at the base of each petal piece, and pinch it together to make a pucker. **J-L**

STEP 7. Add each of the large petal sections to the flower by putting glue into their centers and pressing them into the bottom of the flower, one at a time. **M**

STEP 8. Add additional pigment to the large petals, if desired, with a paintbrush. **N**

STEM, CALYX, AND LEAVES

STEP 1. To add a stem, calyx, and leaves to the Café au Lait Dahlia, see Attach the Stem and Calyx (page 12). **A**

Fall Leaf Branches

Depending on where you live, autumn may or may not grace you with colorful foliage on the trees. Good thing you can create that cozy, fall feeling with felt.

SUPPLIES

9″ × 12″ felt in copper/orange, gold, red, or brown

Fall Leaf template (page 125)

1 piece 18″ long of 18-gauge cloth-covered floral wire

2 pieces 6″ each of 20- or 22-gauge cloth-covered floral wire

Scissors

Hot glue gun and glue sticks

CUT PIECES

Follow the template to cut out

5–7 leaf shapes

CONSTRUCT THE BRANCH

STEP 1. Run a line of glue down the center of one leaf. Press the leaf around a 6˝ piece of 20- or 22-gauge wire. **A-B**

STEP 2. At the base of each leaf, put a tiny dot of glue on either side of the wire on the back, and fold the sides of the leaf back. This will keep the leaf open. **C-D**

STEP 3. Repeat steps 1 and 2 to add a leaf to both ends of both small pieces of wire. Repeat to add the last leaf to the tip of the 18-gauge wire. **E**

STEP 4. Twist one leaf pair onto the main stem, spacing it about 1˝ to 2˝ from the top leaf. Place the main wire in the center of the leaf pair stem. Wrap one side of the small wire around the main wire once or twice. Repeat with the other side. Wrap tightly so that it doesn't slip and spin. Add a tiny dot of glue where the wires meet in the back to give some stability, if needed. **F**

STEP 5. Repeat Step 4 with the second and third leaf pairs. Add additional leaves if desired. **G**

Dried Fern

Fern fronds are lovely and exciting to look at even as they dry out, thanks to their interesting shape and structure. Using wire to create the fern enables it to be curved and shaped into various positions, mimicking the way it would curl in nature as it dries.

SUPPLIES

6″ × 9″ bronze, olive, or brown felt

Dried Fern template (page 125)

1 piece 18″ long of 18-gauge cloth-covered floral wire

Scissors

Hot glue gun and glue sticks

Fabric stiffener

CONSTRUCT THE FERN

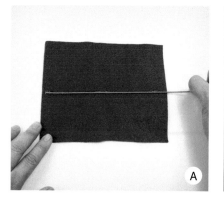

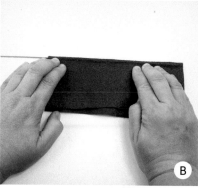

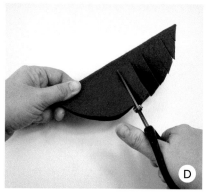

STEP 1. Add a line of glue down the center of the felt rectangle from top to bottom. **A**

STEP 2. Press the wire into the glue, then fold the fern in half and press all along the wire. The wire should be hidden when you open the fern. If it's still showing, add a little more glue where needed, and press again. **B**

STEP 3. Use the Dried Fern template (page 125) as a guide to cut the felt into the shape of a large leaf. **C**

STEP 4. Cut strips, about ¾" apart, perpendicular to the stem wire. Cut close to the wire, within about ½," but not all the way to the wire. Cut through both layers. **D**

STEP 5. Again, cutting through both layers at once, trim the ends of the strips into points to shape the fern. **E**

STEP 6. Spray the fern generously with fabric stiffener. **F**

STEP 7. Use your fingers to curl each of the leaves inward toward the front of the leaf. **G**

STEP 8. Bend the wire into a horizontal "S" curve. **H**

Mini Sunflower

Sunflowers come in more sizes and colors than you may realize! Some types can grow as tall as 30 feet with centers larger than a dinner plate. This delicate take on the sunflower, however, gives us the opportunity to use them in smaller projects and as accent flowers in arrangements. Same sunny disposition, just in a smaller package.

SUPPLIES

12″ × ½″ strip of dark brown felt

4″ × ¾″ piece of light brown felt

6″ × 9″ piece of gold (or other color) felt

6″ × 9″ piece of green felt

Mini Sunflower templates (page 122)

1 piece 18″ long of 18-gauge cloth-covered floral wire

Scissors

Hot glue gun

Glue sticks

CUT PIECES

Follow the template to cut out

15 petals in gold felt

1 calyx in green felt

2 leaves in green felt

CONSTRUCT THE FLOWERS

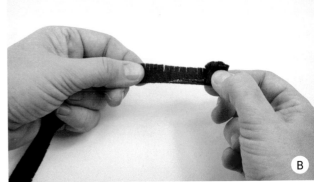

STEP 1. Cut tiny slits along one long side of the dark brown felt, about ⅛" long and ⅛" apart. **A**

STEP 2. Glue along the other uncut long side, and roll the strip up. **B**

STEP 3. Glue along one long edge of the light brown strip, and fold it in half lengthwise. **C**

STEP 4. Attach the light brown piece, folded side up, onto the dark brown center. The folded side of the light brown should be flush with the top of the slits on the dark brown center. Glue into place. **D-E**

STEP 5. Put some glue at the bottom of one petal, and pinch it together. Some glue will press out. Use this extra bit of glue to attach the petal onto the center piece. If no glue squeezes out, add some to the petal before attaching it. **F**

STEP 6. Repeat Step 5 to add the rest of the petals, attaching them side-by-side, all around the center piece. You may not use all 15 petals, or you may need to cut out an extra petal or two depending on how you space them. **G-H**

STEM, CALYX, AND LEAVES

STEP 1. To add a stem, calyx, and leaves to the mini sunflowers, see Attach the Stem and Calyx (page 12). **A**

Wheat

Wheat comes center stage in fall decor. Earthy and neutral, wheat relies on its vertical shape and intricate structure to provide visual interest. Bundle the wheat harvest style, or use a few stems here or there for a minimal look.

SUPPLIES

6˝ × 9˝ tan felt

Wheat templates (page 122)

1 piece 18˝ long of 18-gauge cloth-covered floral wire

Scissors

Hot glue gun and glue sticks

CUT PIECES

Follow the template to cut out

11–15 small wheat pieces from tan felt

4 large wheat pieces from tan felt

CONSTRUCT THE WHEAT

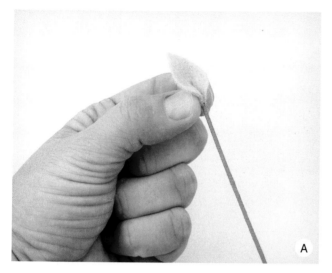

STEP 1. Put a small dot of glue at the base (the rounded end) of a small wheat piece, and press it around the top of the wire. **A**

STEP 2. Repeat Step 1, attaching a piece to the wire on the side of the first. The base of the second piece should touch the base of the first, concealing the wire. Angle the second piece outward so it's sticking out from the wire. Add a third piece opposite the second. **B**

STEP 3. Continue adding the small wheat pieces on either side of the wire, working your way down. Each piece should slightly overlap the previous piece. **C**

STEP 4. Finally, attach the four large pieces below the small pieces using the same method. **D**

STEP 5. Once the glue is set, add some shape to the large pieces by pulling and twisting the tips to give them a thin point. **E**

Bunny Tail

Another favorite in the dried flower world, bunny tails give a neutral, understated texture. Group them together for a fluffy feel, use for filler in a bouquet, or accent with a few stems here and there. Any way you use them, they're undeniably adorable, thanks in part to their name!

SUPPLIES

1˝ x 9˝ strip of off-white felt

1 piece 18˝ long of 18-gauge cloth-covered floral wire

Hot glue gun and glue sticks

White acrylic paint (see Pigments, page 10)

Paintbrush

CONSTRUCT THE BUNNY TAIL

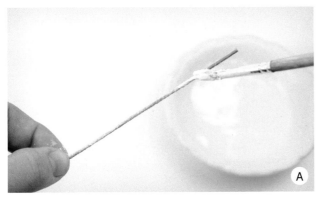

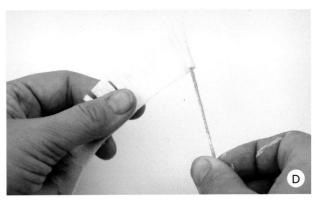

STEP 1. Paint the stem wire with acrylic paint to soften the color. You can buy white wire instead, but if you want to use what you have or don't want stark white, painting is a good option. Let the paint dry completely. **A**

STEP 2. Cut small slits in the off-white felt, going about two-thirds of the way through the piece, all the way down one long side. **B**

STEP 3. Add some glue to the uncut long side of the felt, and wrap it around the tip of the wire. As you wrap the felt, move down the wire to form an oblong shape. **C-E**

STEP 4. Trim any pieces of felt that are too long. You can also trim the fluffy shape into a point at the top. **F**

WINTER

Pinecone

Pinecones show their softer side when made of felt. These seed pods of conifers are commonplace outdoors and in decor. However, a closer look at their spiky, dimensional form can bring about a newfound appreciation for their beauty and complexity. In winter when flowers are scarce, the pinecone is ready to step in.

SUPPLIES

9″ × 12″ brown felt rectangle
1½″ felt ball in a neutral color
Pinecone Templates (page 123)

CUT PIECES

Follow the template to cut out
25–30 arch pieces from the brown felt
1 circle piece from the brown felt

CONSTRUCT THE PINECONE

STEP 1. Put a small dot of glue on the top (rounded) side of an arched piece and pinch it together to form a point. Do this to all of the arched pieces. If some excess glue squeezes out, snip it off with a pair of scissors after it dries. **A**

STEP 2. To create the top of the pinecone, roll up one of the pieces and secure it with hot glue at the bottom. **B**

STEP 3. Add a line of glue to the bottom of another piece and wrap it around the first piece, facing the opposite direction. **C**

STEP 4. Attach two more pieces, opposite one another, and facing the first two. Repeat to attach two more pieces, opposite one another, and facing the opposite direction as the first two sets. **D**

STEP 5. Glue the pinecone top to the felt ball. **E**

STEP 6. Create chains of pointed pieces, linking four or five at a time, by gluing the bottom corners of the pieces into a line, slightly overlapping each piece. **F**

STEP 7. Put glue onto the felt ball just below the base of the top piece, and wrap a chain around the ball. If the chain doesn't go all the way around, that's okay. **G-H**

STEP 8. Keep adding glue to the ball below the previous row and adding all of the chains. Fill in all the gaps on all sides of the ball. All points should face the same direction. **I**

STEP 9. Finish the bottom by gluing on the circle of brown felt to fully cover the ball. **J**

PINECONE ON A STEM

If you're putting the pinecone on a stem, add the stem before Step 9. After adding the wire, use the brown circle in the same way you would add a calyx to a flower. See Attach the Stem and Calyx (page 12).

Poinsettia

The poinsettia is a holiday classic and can be used in so many ways. We'll use fabric stiffener to give strength to the large petals. Though red is the most common color, remember that poinsettias also come in shades of pink and white, so choose the color that works with your holiday decor.

SUPPLIES

9″ x 12″ piece of red felt

1″ x 3″ strip of light green felt

6″ x 9″ piece of green felt

Poinsettia templates (page 123)

1 piece 18″ long of 18-gauge cloth-covered floral wire

Scissors

Hot glue gun and glue sticks

Fabric stiffener

Yellow acrylic paint

Paintbrush

CUT PIECES

Follow the template to cut out

5 large petals in red felt

5 small petals in red felt

2 leaves in green felt

CONSTRUCT THE FLOWER

STEP 1. Spray one large petal generously with fabric spray. **A**

STEP 2. Fold it in half, lengthwise, and press a crease into the center. **B**

STEP 3. Repeat steps 1 and 2 for all large petals, small petals, and leaves. Let them dry completely. **C**

STEP 4. Create the center of the poinsettia. Apply a line of glue down one long side of the light green strip of felt. **D**

STEP 5. Fold it over and press the two sides together. **E**

STEP 6. Cut slits down the folded side, about ⅛″ apart and halfway through the strip. **F**

STEP 7. Put some glue onto one short end of the felt strip and start to wrap it around the stem wire. **G**

STEP 8. Continue wrapping the entire piece around the wire, gluing to secure along the way. Slightly move down the wire as you wrap. **H-I**

STEP 9. Dab yellow acrylic paint onto the loops of the green center for added detail. **J**

STEP 10. Put some glue on the base of a small petal. **K**

STEP 11. Press it onto the bottom of the green center. **L**

STEP 12. Repeat Steps 10 and 11 to attach all five small petals around the center, spacing them evenly. **M**

STEP 13. Add the large petals in the same way, being sure to stagger them in the spaces between the small petals. **N**

STEP 14. Glue the two leaves to the wire directly below the flower, pointing in opposite directions. **O-P**

Camellia

The camellia is one of my longtime favorite flowers. When the cold months set in, camellias keep their shiny green leaves and are among the only flowers to bloom in January.

SUPPLIES

9″ × 12″ fuchsia felt
½″ × 4″ strip of yellow
6″ × 9″ dark green felt
Camellia templates (page 125)
1 piece 18″ long of 18-gauge
cloth-covered floral wire
Hot glue gun and glue sticks
Scissors

CUT PIECES

Follow the template to cut out
12–13 petals from fuchsia felt
2 leaves from green felt
1 calyx from green felt

CONSTRUCT THE FLOWER

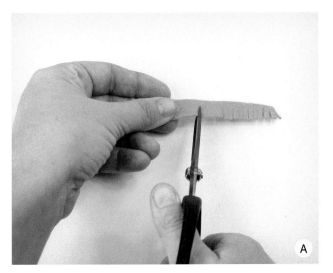

STEP 1. Cut slits along one long side of the yellow felt strip to create a fringe. Cut approximately halfway across the felt and every ⅛″, being careful not to snip the piece in two. **A**

STEP 2. Add glue along the uncut long side of the yellow felt, and roll it up to create the center of the camellia. **B-C**

STEP 3. Cut a ¼″ slit in the top and bottom of three petals. Cut a ¼″ slit in the top only of the remaining petals. **D**

E

F

G

H

STEP 4. Add a bit of glue to one side of a slit, and overlap the other side to create a curve in the petals. The petals with two slits will be overlapped and curved on both sides. The others will just have the overlapped curve on the tops of the petals. **E-F**

STEP 5. Beginning with a petal that's curved on both ends, apply some glue to one end, inside the curve. **G**

STEP 6. Press the petal onto the bottom of the yellow center. **H**

STEP 7. Add the other two double-curved petals in this same way, evenly spacing the three petals around the center. **I**

STEP 8. Add the next five petals. Put glue on the end of the petal that is not curved. Press the petal onto the flower. Position the petal so it's not standing straight up but rather angling out slightly. Space these five petals evenly around the flower.**J**

STEP 9. Add the last five petals in the same way, adding glue to the flat side and spacing them between and behind the previous petals so they're staggered. **K**

STEM, CALYX, AND LEAVES

STEP 1. To add a stem, calyx, and leaves to the camellias, see Attach the Stem and Calyx (page 12). **A**

Holly Branch

With so few flowers blooming in winter, the red berries of the holly plant add some color to our winter foliage. This tutorial makes easy work of the berries by using pre-rolled felt balls.

SUPPLIES

9″ x 12″ green felt

½″ red felt balls

Holly Leaf template (page 125)

1 piece 18″ long of 18-gauge cloth-covered floral wire

Hot glue gun and glue sticks

Scissors

CUT PIECES

Follow the template to cut out
9 holly leaves from green felt

CONSTRUCT THE HOLLY BRANCH

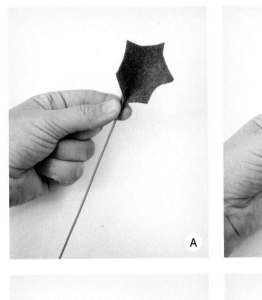

STEP 1. Attach the first leaf to the stem wire by applying a dot of hot glue to the bottom of the leaf and pinching it around the tip of the wire. **A**

STEP 2. Add the next leaf about 1˝ below the first. Position the leaf to the side, then angle it out. **B**

STEP 3. Attach the next leaf in the same way on the opposite side. **C**

STEP 4. Continue adding leaves, in pairs, down the wire stem until you've added all the leaves. **D**

STEP 5. Add the red felt balls to look like berries to the base of several leaves by using a small dot of glue, either on the ball or onto the leaf itself. Use as few or as many as you like! **E-F**

Evergreen

Fresh Evergreen branches may last you through the season, but this felt version lasts even longer! Adding evergreen gives every project a winter-y touch. It's neutral enough to use all winter long and festive enough to pull out for the holidays!

SUPPLIES

18″ × 1½″ dark green felt

Evergreen template (page 125)

1 piece 18″ long of 18-gauge cloth-covered floral wire

Hot glue gun and glue sticks

Scissors

CUT PIECES

Use the template as a guide to cut long, narrow points along one side of the dark green felt strip. This can also be done freehand.

CONSTRUCT THE EVERGREEN

STEP 1. Put a small amount of glue along the edge of the uncut side of the strip, near one short end. **A**

STEP 2. Wrap the felt around the tip of the wire and hold until the glue sets. **B**

STEP 3. Continue adding glue and wrapping the strip around the wire. I suggest adding 2″ to 3″ of glue at a time. Move down the wire as you wrap. Repeat until you get to the end of the felt. **C-D**

Projects

Spring Wreath

This spring wreath is packed full of so many lovely things!
The abundance of blooms and sweet little bees embody the excitement
and cheer that comes with all springtime's abundance.

SUPPLIES

14″ moss-covered wreath base

3 Daffodils (page 25)

2 Jasmine Vines (page 29)

2 Stargazer Lilies (page 18)

3 Icelandic Poppies (page 15)

2 felt bees

2–3 pieces 18″ long of 18-gauge
cloth-covered floral wire

Notes on Construction

The wreath used in this project has a foam base covered in moss. This makes adding the flowers really simple! After you've created all of your blooms, add a stem that's about 2″ long to each one and to the felt bees. This should be long enough to secure the flowers into the wreath without poking all the way through to the other side. You want the flowers to be on the bottom front but also slightly cradled at the base inside curve of the wreath. When the wreath is hanging, the flowers shouldn't stick straight out. When adding the flowers, hold your wreath up from time to time to see how they look. I purchased my felt bees online, but you could also use wool roving to make your own.

CONSTRUCT THE WREATH

STEP 1. Begin with the Stargazer lilies. Position the lilies just to the left of center on the wreath, and press the wire into the foam. Put them close together so they overlap a little. **A**

STEP 2. Add the daffodils. Insert the daffodil stems into the wreath at an angle. Put two to the right of the lilies, and one on the left side. **B**

STEP 3. Add the Icelandic poppies. Again, add two on the right side and one on the left. You can change up the placement on your wreath if you'd like. **C**

STEP 4. Insert a jasmine stem on both sides of the wreath. **D**

STEP 5. Add the bees. Add them to the wreath above the flowers so they appear to be flying. **E-F**

Jasmine Crown

Calling all free spirits and flower girls: A jasmine crown that lasts forever for a delicate touch of springtime, anytime. Tie one on for your next picnic, outdoor event, or dance around the maypole.

SUPPLIES

Brown bark-covered wire
(enough to wrap around the head, plus 3″)

21 individual jasmine flowers
(see Jasmine Vines, page 29)

21 individual jasmine leaves
(see Jasmine Vines, page 29)

21 pieces 4½″ each of 22-gauge wire

Twine or ribbon for tying

CONSTRUCT THE CROWN

STEP 1. Add a jasmine flower to one end of each of the small pieces of wire. Add a leaf to the other end (refer to the jasmine instructions on page 29). Bundle them into groups of two and three by twisting the wires together. **A**

STEP 2. Assemble the crown base. Twist the wire to create a loop on both ends of the bark-wrapped wire. **B**

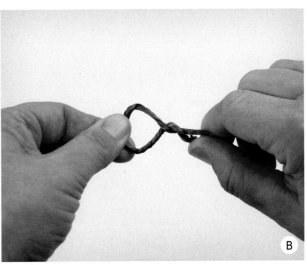

STEP 3. Add the jasmine bundles to the crown base. Start by tightly twisting a bundle of three jasmines around the wire of the crown base, with the blooms facing one end of the crown. Then add a bundle of two to the crown base. Bend the leaves up toward and around the blooms. **C-D**

STEP 4. Continue adding jasmine bundles, alternating between bundles of two and three until you reach the other end of the base. **E-F**

STEP 5. Thread the twine through both loops on the crown and tie it into a bow. You can adjust the size of the crown by tying it tighter or looser. **G**

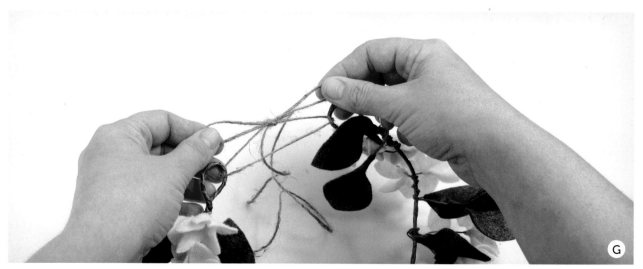

Foraged Wreath

Imagine the mossy forest floor as a wreath! I imagine faeries and gnomes hiding behind the fallen pine cones and resting under the mushrooms. All of the elements featured on this wreath could be found on a nature walk. This wreath works great as decor in both summer and fall.

SUPPLIES

Grapevine wreath base

Sheet moss 4″ to 5″ long and 3″ wide,
or enough to wrap a 4″ section
around bottom of wreath

6 Dried Ferns (page 59)
attached to 9″ wires

2 Dried Ferns (page 59)
each attached to the ends of one 18″ wire

Pinecone (page 69) on 2″ to 3″ wire stem

6 Bunny Tails (page 66) attached to 9″ wires

3 Mushrooms (page 49)

18″ piece of cloth-covered floral wire
20-gauge or higher

Scissors

Hot glue gun and glue sticks

CONSTRUCT THE WREATH

STEP 1. Make bundles of "foraged" elements. Gather three ferns, two bunny tails, and the pinecone, and twist the wires together. **A**

STEP 2. Use one of the stems from the bundle to wrap closely around all the other stems to secure. **B**

STEP 3. Create a second bundle by wrapping three ferns and four bunny tails together. Don't use the double-ended fern. **C**

STEP 4. Put both bundles end to end, with stems facing one another, and twist their wires together to make a two-sided bundle. Use the double-ended fern on the long stem to wrap around the twisted stems, securing them further. **D-E**

STEP 5. Place the large bundle onto the wreath base. Use the 18″ floral wire to wrap the bundle onto the wreath. **F**

STEP 6. Trim the sheet moss to approximately the length of the stems between the foliage. Make sure you have a piece large enough to wrap around the thickness of the wreath. The exact size will vary depending on how far apart the foliage is and the size of the wreath base. **G**

STEP 7. Use hot glue to attach the moss to the wreath base. Use a generous amount of glue and wrap the moss all the way around the wreath. Be sure the seam, where the two ends of moss meet, is positioned on the back of the wreath so it doesn't show. **H**

STEP 8. Add the mushrooms. Put some glue on the bottom of a mushroom stem and press it directly onto the sheet moss in the desired location. **I-J**

STEP 9. Repeat to add the rest of the mushrooms. **K**

Autumnal Garland

This garland brings the colors and warmth of fall anywhere you put it. Hang it over a door or down the center of a table. It can easily be made longer by using a longer piece of bark-wrapped wire and adding more bundles.

SUPPLIES

5 Fall Leaf Branches (page 57)

5 Wheat (page 64)

10 Bunny Tails (page 66)

5 Mini Sunflowers (page 61)

Bark-wrapped wire, at least 3′

Jute twine about 4′ to 5′

Scissors

CONSTRUCT THE GARLAND

STEP 1. Create five bundles of flowers and foliage, each containing one fall branch, one wheat, two bunny tails, and one mini sunflower. Arrange so the plants are staggered by height, as shown, and twist the stems together to hold. **A**

STEP 2. Trim the stems so there are about 1½″ of twisted stems on the bottom of each bundle. **B-C**

STEP 3. Create a loop at each end of the bark-wrapped wire (the garland base) and twist. You'll use these loops to hang the finished garland. **D**

STEP 4. Begin to add the bundles to the garland base wire. Use a piece of jute twine to tie each bundle onto the garland base. Leave a little twine tail hanging off the knot. **E**

STEP 5. Wrap a new piece of twine all the way down the stems and back up again. Secure the twine by tying it off to the little tail you left. Trim. **F**

STEP 6. Add the next bundle to the garland base so that the tops of the fall leaves meet the bottom of the sunflower. Repeat steps 4 and 5 to attach. **G**

STEP 7. Repeat steps 4–6 until you've added all the bundles. If you find your bundles need extra security, use some twine to tie the leaf branches to the garland base. **H**

Sunflower Headband

A cheery sunflower headband is enough to brighten even the chilliest fall day!
You'll use a nylon headband in this project that's super soft and stretchy,
making it perfect for the sunflower lover of any age.

SUPPLIES

Thin nylon headband

3 mini sunflowers (page 61)

4 jasmine leaves (page 123) in sage green felt

4½″ × 2″ strip of sage green felt

1 book (to stretch headband around)

CONSTRUCT THE HEADBAND

STEP 1. To make the stretchy headband easier to work with, stretch it over a book while you're working. Place the green strip of felt under the headband. Put a line of glue down one edge of the felt. **A**

STEP 2. Fold the felt over and press the two sides together. Make sure the glue doesn't get on the headband. It should be able to move freely within the felt tunnel. **B**

STEP 3. Glue a leaf on both ends of the felt strip, points facing the headband. **C**

STEP 4. Put glue on the back of a sunflower, and attach it over the inside end of one of the leaves. **D**

STEP 5. Attach the second flower on the opposite side in the same way. **E**

STEP 6. Attach two leaves onto the third flower by gluing them to the bottom, facing opposite directions. **F**

STEP 7. Glue the third flower and the leaves into the center of the felt strip. **G-H**

Woodland Cloche

A tiny moment found on the woodland floor is captured and on display in this cloche project. Wool roving emulates the mossy ground where a family of mushrooms gathers under the ferns.

SUPPLIES

8″ cloche with wooden base

3 Mushrooms (page 49)

2 Dried Ferns (page 59)
on 1″ long cloth-covered wires

1 ounce of wool roving in olive green

Styrofoam square about 2″ × 2″ × ½″

Hot glue gun and glue sticks

FILL THE CLOCHE

STEP 1. Add a little glue to the center base of the cloche. **A**

STEP 2. Press a small piece of Styrofoam onto it. This is a good opportunity to reuse some Styrofoam that you may have lying around from packaging instead of buying Styrofoam or floral foam new. **B**

STEP 3. Add glue all around the outside of the foam. Press and wrap the wool roving onto the foam, covering it. Add more glue and arrange until you can't see the foam. You may have extra wool roving left over to use in another project. **C**

STEP 4. Decide where you would like to place the mushrooms. Adjust the roving to make a gap through to the foam, add glue, and firmly press the mushroom stem into the glue. Repeat to add the other mushrooms. **D-E**

STEP 5. Stick the dried ferns into the foam, through the roving, behind the mushrooms. Place the cloche top over the greenery. **F**

Evergreen Swag

This evergreen swag is a great winter accent to bring nature in for the season. Use alone as an understated holiday decoration, or group several together on a tabletop, across a mantle, or attached to the back of dining room chairs.

SUPPLIES

5 double-sided Evergreens (page 82)
on 9˝ wires

2 Evergreens (page 82) on 18˝ wires

1 double-sided Pinecone (page 69)
on a 6˝ wire

½˝ off-white felt balls (optional)

Wire snips

Hot glue gun and glue sticks (optional)

CONSTRUCT THE SWAG

STEP 1. Twist a double-sided evergreen stem onto one of the 18˝ evergreens. Wrap it securely just below the single evergreen around until the base of the greenery touches the main wire. **A**

STEP 2. Add a second double-sided evergreen stem 1˝ below the first one, wrapping in the same way. **B**

STEP 3. Repeat steps 1 and 2 to create a second evergreen branch. **C**

STEP 4. Join the two branches by twisting them together just below the greenery. **D**

STEP 5. Trim the extra wire with a pair of wire snips. **E**

STEP 6. Add the pinecones by wrapping the double-ended pinecone stem around the middle of the swag where the evergreen branches were joined. Wrap until the bottoms of the pinecones touch the swag. **F**

STEP 7. Create a loop in the last double-sided evergreen stem. Wrap it around the middle of the swag. You'll use the loop to hang the swag, and the extra evergreen gives it additional fullness. **G-H**

STEP 8. If desired, use hot glue to attach felt balls directly to the swag to look like berries. **I**

Candle Circlet

Spruce up your favorite candle for the winter days by creating a festive circle of holly and poinsettias. The jar candle used in this project is exceptionally large; however, you can adjust the size of your circlet easily by using fewer or more holly branches. This can be adapted to wrap around a large pillar candle or even a cluster of battery-operated taper candles.

SUPPLIES

8 Holly Branches (page 80) on 18″ stems

3 Poinsettias (page 72) without stems

Candle (optional)

CONSTRUCT THE CIRCLET

STEP 1. Twist the stems of two holly branches together so that one is about 3″ to 4″ higher than the other. **A**

STEP 2. Add another branch to the bundle so the top is 3″ to 4″ below the lowest branch. **B**

STEP 3. Continue connecting holly branches until the combined stem is long enough to wrap all the way around a candle or dish. Leave one holly left over. **C**

STEP 4. Form the holly into a circle, and twist the end of the final unused holly around the first branch where they meet. **D**

STEP 5. Position the stems so they're tucked in and not sticking out. Bend leaves of some of the holly branches so they're poking out a little in different directions. **E**

STEP 6. Put glue on the back of a poinsettia and press it into a holly leaf near the stem. Add the remaining two poinsettias around the circle. **F-G**

Potted Plant

Make this plant as large or as small as you want! Add more leaves to fill it out, or keep it simple with the five used in the instructions. The gradient of leaf color gives the smallest leaves the impression of new growth.

SUPPLIES

Planter or pot

2 Monstera leaves (page 36) on
18˝ wire stems in dark green felt

2 medium Monstera leaves (page 36) on
18˝ wire stems in medium green felt

1 small Monstera leaf (page 36) on an
18˝ wire stem in light green

1˝ × 2˝ strip of light green felt

1 block Styrofoam or floral foam large
enough to fit snugly into your planter

Wire snips

Gravel

Hot glue gun and glue sticks

Resizing the Monstera template

To create small- and medium-sized monstera
leaves, resize the Monstera template (page 124).
For the medium leaf, reduce the template to 75%
of the original size. For the small leaf, reduce the
template to 50% of the original size.

ASSEMBLE THE PLANT

STEP 1. Begin by twisting the large leaves together at the
bottom of the stems. Twist on the medium leaves above
the large leaves, and then the smallest leaf at the top. A-B

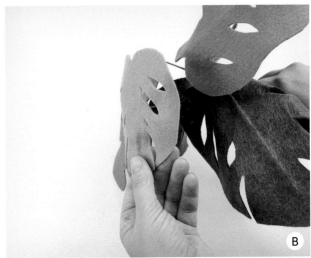

STEP 2. Use a wire from one of the stems to wrap all of the stems together more tightly. **C**

STEP 3. Trim the wires with a pair of wire cutters to even them off. **D**

STEP 4. Use the strip of felt to cover the stems at the base of the plant, just below the leaves where the wires are twisted. Add hot glue to the felt and fold it over and around the wires longways. Trim the excess felt with scissors. **E-F**

STEP 5. Cut down the foam so it fits inside the planter or pot. This is a good opportunity to reuse some Styrofoam that you may have lying around from packaging instead of buying Styrofoam or floral foam new. The foam needs to fit snugly in the planter and fill it up about ¾ of the way. **G**

STEP 6. Poke a hole in the foam and stick the plant in it so no wires are showing. Fill the hole with hot glue and hold the plant upright until the glue sets. **H**

STEP 7. Fill the planter with gravel. The gravel will fill in all the gaps, cover the foam, and add weight to the plant so it doesn't fall over. **I**

STEP 8. Arrange the leaves of the plant by bending the wire at the base of each leaf. **J**

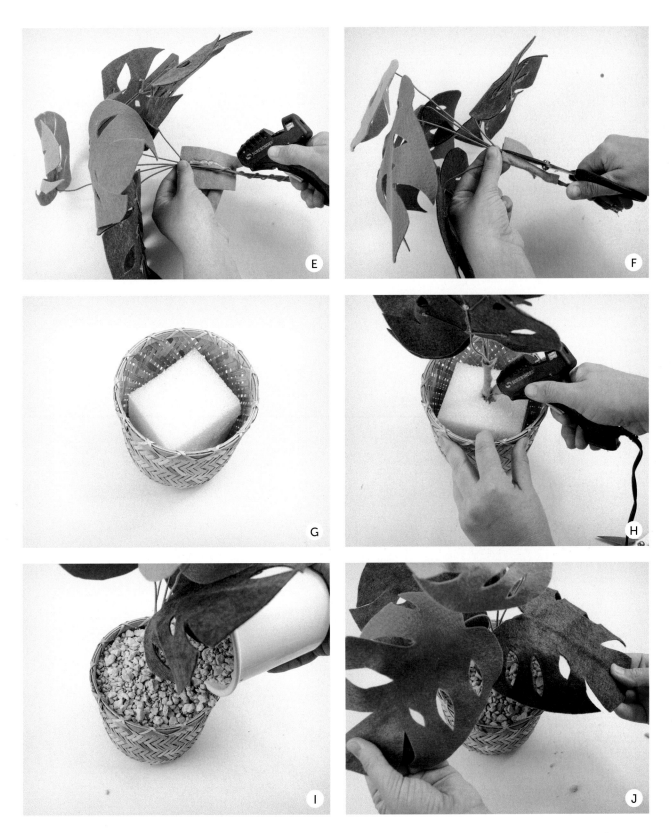

Tropical Centerpiece

This asymmetric arrangement highlights the bold colors and
geometric shapes of the blooms and foliage used to create it.
If you can't be on vacation all the time, bring it to your home or event
with these saturated hues and striking silhouettes.

SUPPLIES

Pot or vessel about 4″ wide x 5″ tall

1 Monstera leaf (page 36)

1 Palm Fan (page 46)

1 Protea (page 41)

4 Hibiscus in two colors (page 33)

Chicken wire

CONSTRUCT THE CENTERPIECE

STEP 1. Create a spherical shape with the chicken wire. This should be a rough, rounded shape. Work the wire in sections to get the round shape until it's about the right size to fit snugly into the pot or vessel. The chicken wire will hold the stems in place, giving them structure. **A-B**

STEP 2. Begin with the palm frond and monstera leaf. The palm will be the highest point, and the monstera will be the lowest point. Trim the stem of the palm to the desired height, ensuring it's long enough to stand up higher than the vessel. Insert the stem at an angle so it is supported by the chicken wire. You can adjust the length of the stem by trimming extra if needed. Add the monstera at a diagonal on the opposite side. **C-D**

STEP 3. Place the hibiscus blooms. Trim and insert them on an angle in between both leaves. **E**

STEP 4. Add the other two hibiscus blooms and the protea. Play around with the placement so that the chicken wire and the stem wires aren't visible. Check the arrangement from all sides to see if there are any empty spaces that need filling. Adjust the positioning of the flowers as needed. If you're noticing gaps that you can't fill by changing the arrangement, add more flowers. **F-G**

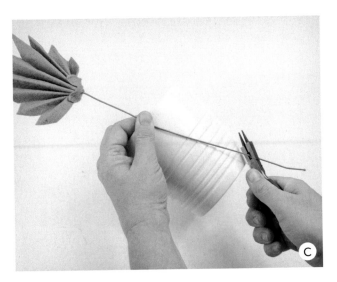

Bouquet

The subtle differences in color of the blooms in this neutral bouquet highlight the texture of each bloom. The muted color pallet and chiffon ribbon set a soft and romantic mood for a dreamy special day. This bouquet utilizes flowers from multiple seasons because no flower is out of season when it's made of felt!

SUPPLIES

2 Claire de Lune Peonies on
18˝ wire stems (page 22)

2 Café au Lait Dahlias on
18˝ wire stems (page 53)

2 Camellias in an off-white color on
18˝ wire stems (page 76)

2 Bunny Tails on 18˝ wire stems (page 66)

3 Dried Ferns on 18˝ wire stems (page 59)

12 stems of basic greenery on
18˝ wire stems (see below)

1 yard (approx.) of chiffon ribbon
in mauve

GREENERY

*Create basic greenery by cutting out
5–6 green leaves per greenery stem, using
the jasmine leaf template. Add glue to the tips
and pinch them around a piece of stem wire.
Begin by gluing the first leaf to the very tip of
the wire. Then glue and pinch leaves down the
stem wire, alternating adding them to the left
and right sides of the wire.*

CONSTRUCT THE BOUQUET

STEP 1. Begin by holding the dahlias in one hand. Stagger the blooms, one higher than the other. Bend the wire where it meets the flower head so the flowers are facing toward you. **A**

STEP 2. Add the camellias next. Again, stagger one higher than the other and face the blooms to you slightly. **B**

A

B

STEP 3. Add one Claire de Lune to the top left and the other to the bottom right. **C**

TIP

Keep in mind, the exact placement of the flowers can be adjusted as you go along since they're on wires. It's easy to reposition flowers to get the desired appearance.

STEP 4. Add the greenery stems. Gather five greenery stems and add them to the right side of the arrangement at about a 45° angle. **D**

STEP 5. Gather four greenery stems and add them to the left side of the bouquet, still at an angle, but slightly lower. We want to keep this bouquet balanced but not completely symmetrical. **E**

STEP 6. Insert 2–3 pieces of greenery between the flowers in the bouquet to create some separation and contrast between blooms. **F**

STEP 7. Spread apart the greenery stems on the sides, and position them around the sides of the arrangement. Keep the top of the bouquet mostly free of greenery. **G**

STEP 8. Add the two bunny tails to the right side of the bouquet, at an angle so they're sticking out higher than the other flowers. **H**

STEP 9. Place two ferns on the right side and one fern on the left side. **I**

STEP 10. Make adjustments to the flowers and leaves so all the flowers are visible and spaced nicely without too much overlap. The flowers in the back should be higher than the flowers in the front, and the flowers should be positioned so that most of their faces are pointing forward.

STEP 11. When all of the stems are positioned, use a wire from one of the flowers to wrap the stems together. Next, grab all of the wires at the bottom of the bouquet and bend them back up onto themselves about 8″ to 9″ from the lowest flower. **J**

STEP 12. Wrap the stems with ribbon. Beginning at the base of the bouquet, leave about 1′ of ribbon free at the end and wrap the chiffon ribbon all the way down the stems and back up again, fully covering the wires. When the ribbon reaches back to the base where you started wrapping, tie a knot and bow with the two ends. **K-M**

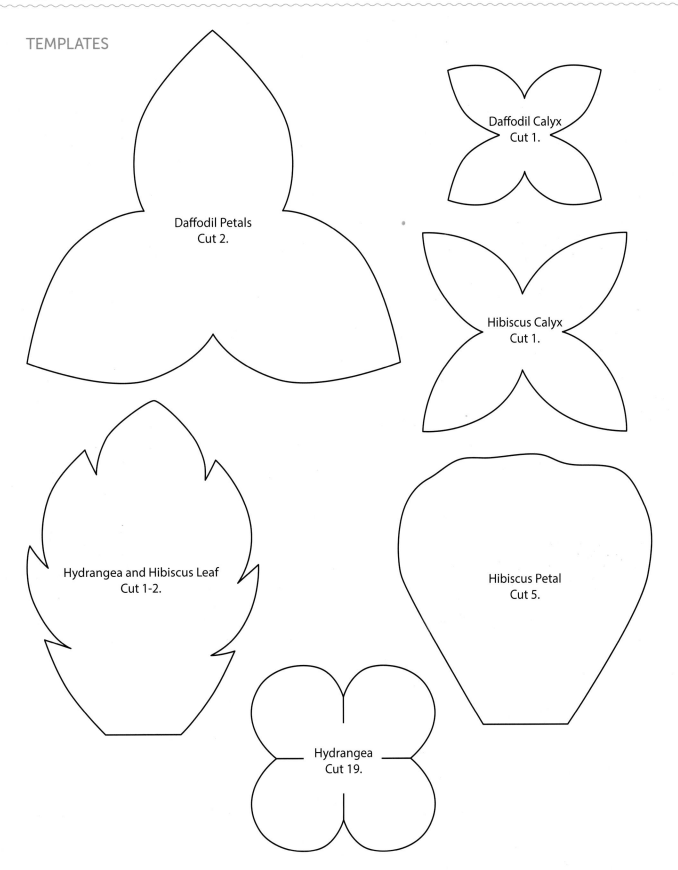

Daffodil Petals
Cut 2.

Daffodil Calyx
Cut 1.

Hibiscus Calyx
Cut 1.

Hydrangea and Hibiscus Leaf
Cut 1-2.

Hibiscus Petal
Cut 5.

Hydrangea
Cut 19.

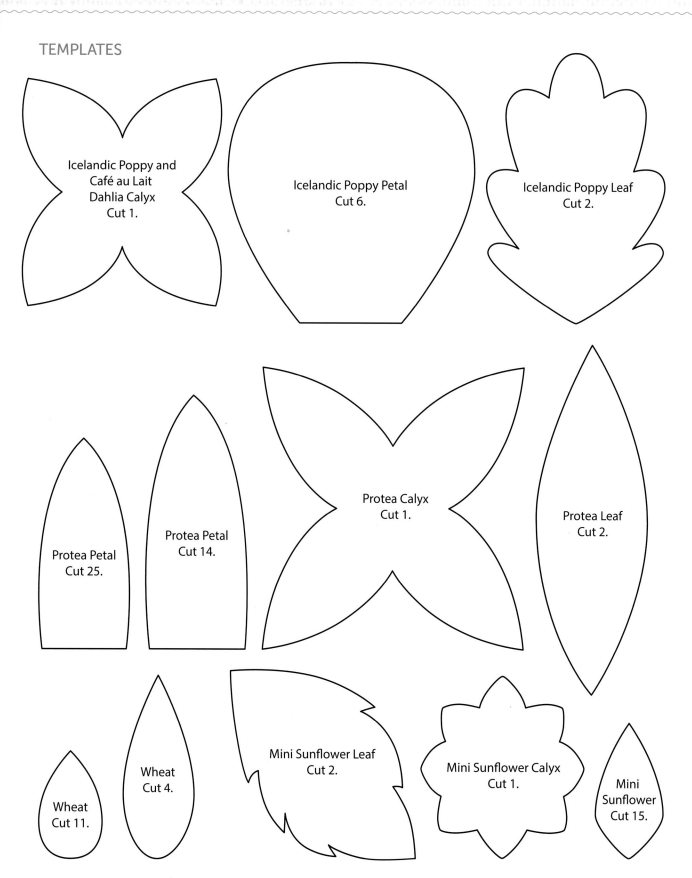

Icelandic Poppy and Café au Lait Dahlia Calyx Cut 1.

Icelandic Poppy Petal Cut 6.

Icelandic Poppy Leaf Cut 2.

Protea Petal Cut 25.

Protea Petal Cut 14.

Protea Calyx Cut 1.

Protea Leaf Cut 2.

Wheat Cut 11.

Wheat Cut 4.

Mini Sunflower Leaf Cut 2.

Mini Sunflower Calyx Cut 1.

Mini Sunflower Cut 15.

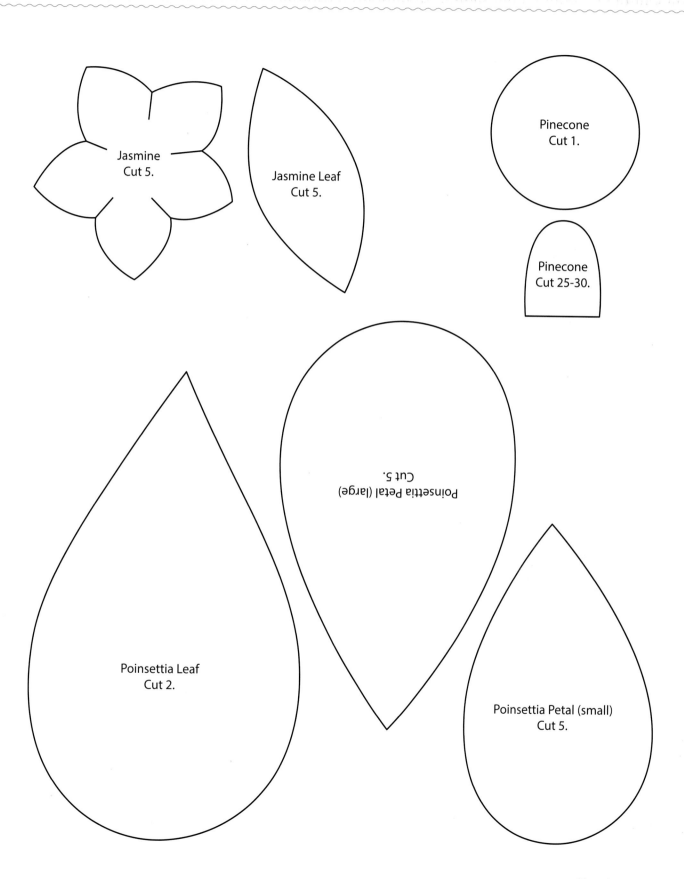

Jasmine
Cut 5.

Jasmine Leaf
Cut 5.

Pinecone
Cut 1.

Pinecone
Cut 25-30.

Poinsettia Petal (large)
Cut 5.

Poinsettia Leaf
Cut 2.

Poinsettia Petal (small)
Cut 5.

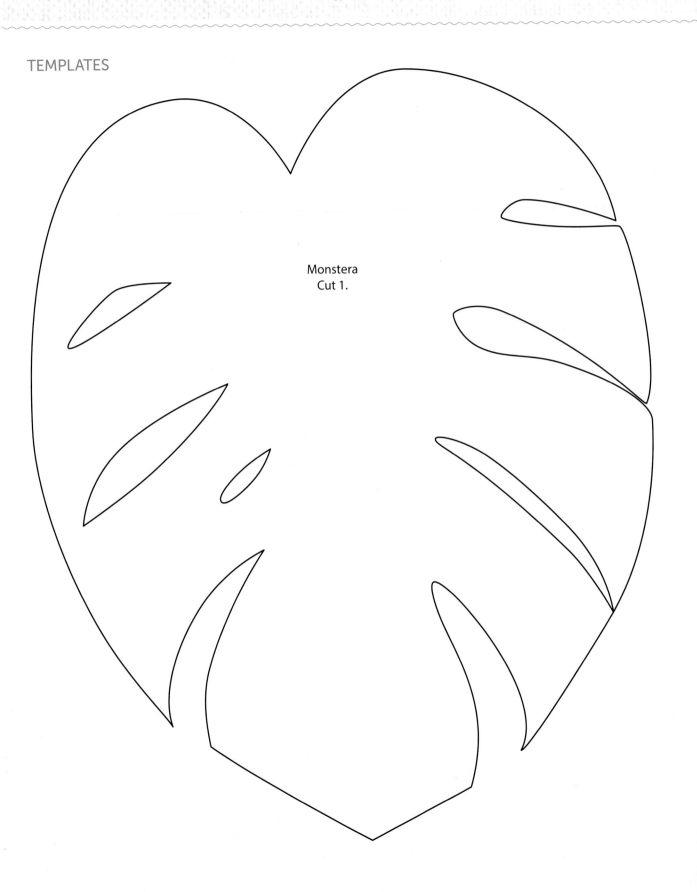

Monstera
Cut 1.

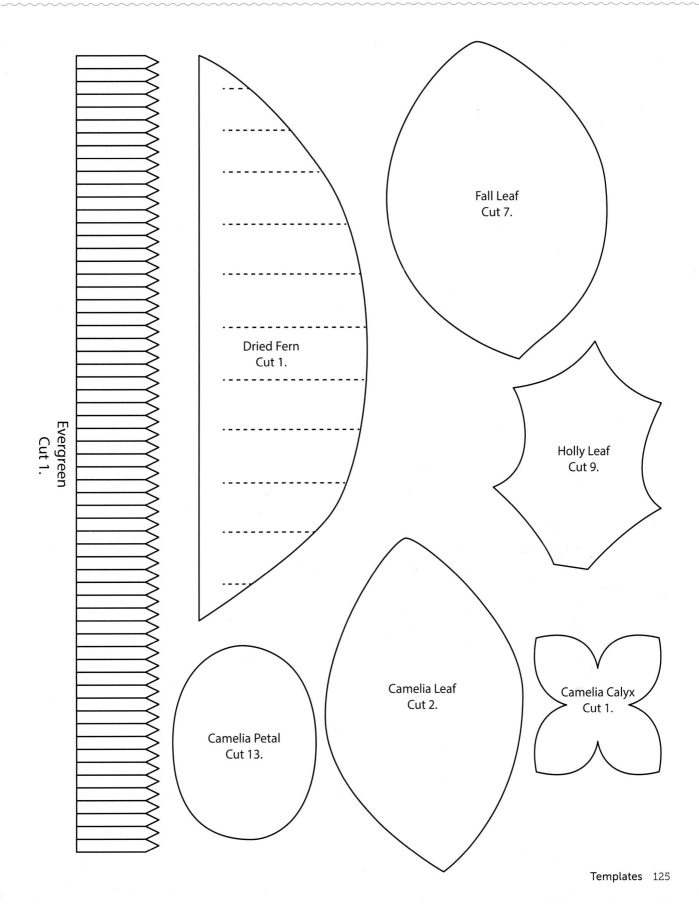

Evergreen
Cut 1.

Dried Fern
Cut 1.

Fall Leaf
Cut 7.

Holly Leaf
Cut 9.

Camelia Petal
Cut 13.

Camelia Leaf
Cut 2.

Camelia Calyx
Cut 1.

TEMPLATES

Stargazer
Calyx
Cut 1.

Claire de Lune
Peony Leaf
Cut 2.

Stargazer
Pollen
Cut 6.

Claire de Lune
Peony Calyx
Cut 1.

Stargazer
Petal
Cut 6.

Stargazer
Cut 1.

Claire de Lune Peony
Size A
Cut 3.

Café au Lait Dahlia (small)
Cut 1.

Claire de Lune Peony
Size B
Cut 3.

Café au Lait Dahlia (large)
Cut 2.

Café au Lait Dahlia Leaf
Cut 1.

Café au Lait Dahlia (medium)
Cut 2.

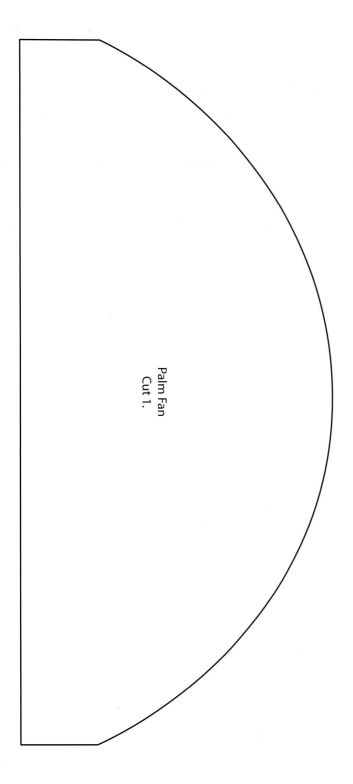

Palm Fan
Cut 1.

ABOUT THE AUTHOR

Bryanne Rajamannar is an artistic entrepreneur and the flower-loving creative force behind Fleurish Felt Flower Co. She holds a Bachelor of Fine Arts degree from Jacksonville University and has studied interior design. She left her corporate job in 2010 after the birth of her first daughter, who became the inspiration for her company.

Bryanne has a brick and mortar shop, a popular Etsy Shop, and her work has appeared in Southwest Magazine, Women's World Magazine, and Jacksonville Magazine. She is the author of *Felt Flower Workshop.*

Bryanne lives in Jacksonville, FL, with her husband and two daughters. Follow along with her @fleurishfeltflowerco on Instagram and fleurishfeltflowerco.com.